COUNTDOWN

Carole Satyamurti is a poet and sociologist, who lives and works in London. For many years she taught at the Tavistock Clinic, where her main academic interest was in the relevance of psychoanalytic ideas to an understanding of the stories people tell about themselves, whether in formal autobiography or in social encounters. She co-edited *Acquainted with the Night: psychoanalysis and the poetic imagination* (2003). She won the National Poetry Competition in 1986, and a Cholmondeley Award in 2000.

Countdown (Bloodaxe Books, 2011) is her first new collection since *Stitching the Dark: New & Selected Poems* (Bloodaxe Books, 2005), which drew on five collections: *Broken Moon* (1987), *Changing the Subject* (1990), *Striking Distance* (1994), *Love and Variations* (2000), and *Stitching the Dark* (2005), two of these Poetry Book Society Recommendations. Her translation from the *Mahabharata* is forthcoming from Norton.

CAROLE SATYAMURTI

COUNTDOWN

BLOODAXE BOOKS

ISBN: 978 1 85224 912 0

First published 2011 by
Bloodaxe Books Ltd,
Highgreen,
Tarset,
Northumberland NE48 1RP.

www.bloodaxebooks.com
For further information about Bloodaxe titles
please visit our website or write to
the above address for a catalogue.

Supported by
**ARTS COUNCIL
ENGLAND**

Cover design: Neil Astley & Pamela Robertson-Pearce.

Printed in Great Britain by
Bell & Bain Limited, Glasgow, Scotland.

ACKNOWLEDGEMENTS

Thanks are due to the editors of the following publications in which some of these poems first appeared: *Ambit*, *Chimera*, *French Literary Review*, *The Frogmore Papers*, *The Guardian*, *Hazy Moon*, *Illuminations*, *The Interpreter's House*, *London Magazine*, *Modern Poetry in Translation*, *Peace News*, *Poetry London*, *Poetry pf website*, *Poetry Review*, *The Rialto*, *Stand*, *Stimulus Respond* and *To Hell With Journals*.

'The Day I Knew I Wouldn't Live For Ever', first published in *The Interpreter's House*, was shortlisted for the Forward Prize for Best Individual Poem, in 2008, and appeared in *The Forward Book of Poetry, 2009*.

I am grateful to the following people who read and commented on individual poems: David Black, Patrick Early, Susanne Ehrhardt, Judy Gahagan, Judith Kazantzis, Mimi Khalvati, Emma Satyamurti, Martin Wilkinson.

Special thanks are due to Gregory Warren Wilson, to whom this book is dedicated.

CONTENTS

III Small Shift

I
COUNTING

The Igneous Age

Naked eyes are dangerous;
a look is a touch is a bitter offence
glances can get you slashed

a gesture might be fatal.
Tinder sticks, too close for cool
strike sparks out of each other;

football grounds are war zones,
the stakes too desperate, bodies
fortified against, always against.

What voice for love on festering estates
where fruits and syrups, wasted long ago,
have fermented to combustion point?

Although on the occasional street corner
you see men chatting, bellies shaking,
you know they must be from elsewhere.

Guns are flourishing in the high-rises.
At night, wanton fires ravage office blocks,
light up the waterfront with blitz.

If someone had a telescope on Mars
would they see some hope in it,
rebirth, perhaps? Or are we lost?

The great protector strutting to the rescue
is besotted with incendiary harm.
The puppet sucks his thumb.

Memorial

This is the house that Jacques built.

This is the tree in the sun-scorched yard
of the weather-proof house that Jacques built.

This is the car, all lacy with rust,
that waits by the linden tree in the yard
of the thick-walled house that Jacques built.

This is the baker, his bread long lost,
who was proud of the car now crumbled with rust
that slumps by the tree in the dusty yard
of the ruined house that Jacques built.

These are the children and neighbours and wives
all dead, like the baker whose life was lost,
who polished the car, now papery rust
like the oven that stands in the silent yard
of the roofless house that Jacques built.

This is the church and the blistered Christ
who couldn't protect the children and wives
who choked in each other's arms, all lost
like the prosperous baker whose car is rust
whose oven stands gaping in the yard
of the desolate house that Jacques built.

These are the soldiers who barred the doors
and torched the Christ; who erased the lives
of the more than six hundred children and wives
and men like the baker, a whole village lost
leaving prams and sewing machines to rust,
bright orange against the dust of the yards
and the stones of the houses Jacques built.

What happened later to minds as split
as those of the soldiers who locked the doors,
Christians, who extinguished the lives
of the more than six hundred children and wives
and men who had plans and loves – all lost;
and the only sign that they lived is rust
on the pans and irons in the rooms and yards
of all the houses Jacques built?

How can the linden tree still flower
from the death-soaked earth of Oradour;
and water from the well run clear,
and bees make harmony every year,
and ants run feckless over the floor?
Just as they do in Sobibor,
Haditha, Shattila, Warsaw,
in Srebrenica and Darfur...

That's how it is in Oradour.

Counting

February, 2003

Paris

A single helicopter, tacking low.
Frosted ivy, cemetery wall;
on top, complacent birds, a pushy row
of witnesses, impassive, as we all

jostled past – a river of us walking –
some of the world's millions saying *No
to War!* that day; all ages marching, talking
with strangers. From Madrid to Tokyo,

today we'd count. Pigeons shrugged, blinking
as if they knew best how things really are.
But I felt we'd win; I remember thinking
they'll have to listen now! And yet, how far

we were from where the eagle turned its head,
preparing to discount the senseless dead.

London

Terror... Evil... National Security.
We're offered rhetoric on paper plates.
We shout in kind, *Not in our name.*

I think – we have no names,
we're alphabet soup, easily digested,
shuffling along on spaghetti legs,
fists light as prawn crackers.

Their names begin with B:
B for bully. B for ballistic
and bomb and bullshit.

This is mirror country where *truly... honestly*
break up on impact. Our leaders
wrap themselves in steel, making H words:
H for headlines, horror, homicide. History.

We're so very biddable. Jolly songs,
right-on badges, getting home for the News.
We want the bone and gristle, the spring
that could turn the world even a few degrees.

I think of Abdul, who will never go home;
of Farah, whose singing days are over, whose flesh
will not, now, age slowly in its living silk.

It's five below. Our numb feet will tramp unheard
down streets of closed doors, shuttered minds.
But stay out a little longer, turn out next time
because – what else? Write a poem?

The Night I Bit George W

There was some ceremony,
and I was to kiss him on those lips
that look as though he's spent a lifetime hooting.

I'd get to eat his words, since he wouldn't.
My teeth felt that tickling sensation
they get after the dentist, or just before
you go berserk and lose it utterly.

I aimed for the lower one – surprisingly salty
tough as squid – and I gnawed
and gnawed, but the flesh seemed irreducible;
then when I gave up, drew away, he was
a rubber manikin, waving, smiling as ever,
and my mouth was slippery with blood.

Innocent Civilian

don't blame me

all I want's a quiet life is that too much to

this is a democracy

this is a peaceful country

if they don't like it they should

no one could call me racist

if they behaved like us I wouldn't even

nothing to do with me

they wouldn't cross my mind

well what *about* it –

I don't even know where it is

I don't understand politics

this is a democracy

don't blame me – I didn't

vote for this government

I didn't even vote

Terror

Now the Shabanites are living in our city
you can't be too careful.
They're everywhere.

What does a Shabanite look like?

Like anyone – friendly, shakes your hand
but you soon know you've met one.

How?

Your skin starts to burn and crack. I've heard
one man's hand shrivelled and fell off.

Have you ever seen one?

I might have – you never know
who's standing next to you.
A few months back, my cousin's sister-in-law
was queuing for fish. The man behind
smiled at her – and she realised, and ran!

What if you never look a stranger in the eye,
what if you keep your hands in your pockets?

I told you – they're everywhere.
Your dentist might be one,
the check-out girl, poisoning your change.

But didn't I hear they tracked down
the last Shabanite – beat him to death?

Well, but what about the Shakuni? I'm told
they operate in cells, have horrible cold breath.
They're everywhere.

Battle Lines

They wear the same boots, the same touching hair-cuts,
they're smiles on the News, digits on print-out,
our brave boys;
names, ranks and numbers, action men
splitting the night with mind-trash noise.

Below them, the lights are the Fourth of July,
the screen shows cursors falling, converging
on other men –
abstract enemies with blanks for faces.
The mission's to smash them and smash them again.

Each leader works at poses, inflections:
strong on screen, bluff on the air-waves,
caring friend.
Each of them bathes in his own propaganda;
his currency's lives, and he's plenty to spend.

It's no use praying for some clean ending,
the God of the cross, of the star, of the crescent
is deaf and blind.
The fall-back, an echo of voices from childhood:
Don't cry big boys. Never mind.

The Legend of the Dead Soldier

a version of Bertolt Brecht's Die Legende vom toten Soldaten

The third year of the war had brought
   no peace or compromise
so the soldier did the expected thing
   and died as a hero dies.

But since the war was not yet won
   the Head of State felt sorry
when his soldier died as a hero dies –
   it seemed a little early.

Summer sweltered over the grave
   on the outskirts of the city.
Then the Head of State called out the army
   medical committee

who marched off to the cemetery
   with army issue tools
and dug up the dead corporal;
   they did it by the rules –

the doctor examined the rotting corpse
   (it wasn't a thing of beauty)
and judged that he was fit to serve –
   just shirking a soldier's duty.

So they hauled him off to the nearby camp.
   The night was clear and calm
and the same stars glittered over the field
   as over the fields back home.

They drenched him in formaldehyde
    and dressed him nice and trim
and made two brawny orderlies
    walk either side of him

to prop him up, while the band blared out
    and dogs and children fought
to see the damaged soldier swing
    his legs as he'd been taught.

In front of him, the flag was spread,
    the spangled red–white–blue,
to rouse his comrades' fighting zeal
    and hide his state from view.

They marched him down the highway
    to the sound of *tan-tara!*
the trees bowed down, the full moon shone
    and the people yelled *hurrah!*

Soon, such was the dancing all around,
    so great were the noise and dust
that no one noticed the poor dead hero
    dragging and staggering past.

Only the stars could see him
    and the stars know very well
that heroes die a thousand deaths
    and each of them is hell.

Bound for Glory

The short biography of an anger starts in the black box
where some hurt, a state of grace destroyed,
scored its mark on an impressionable heart.

We move to Stop and Search, or *News at Ten*;
the anger goes underground, hides at the margins,
the back of the crowd, crusted with insults, hate.

It's homeless, shelters where it can, longing,
searches out a bookshop, a teacher, finding itself
welcome. It sets up camp in the defining story but –

now we re-enter the black box where (we can only guess)
the anger grows muscular enough to throttle itself
and sees, at last, a funnel future opening into light.

Approaching Zero

One hundred and fifty-two steps
from here to there.
Soon the damson tree will drop its fruit.
She notices tiny red spots
on the iron railings.
One hundred and three.
Rust. One thought at a time.
It helps that God has affirmed her,
chapter and verse.
Eighty-four.
To make ready, she has shucked
the whole world of objects.
Thirty-nine. Thirty-eight.
Her feet are walking her,
the enormous consummation
simply one plus one plus one.
Behind her, a life ago, mangled
shirts on the line;
but she will never weep again, never
eat, drink, sleep again. Nor will the passengers.
In the blaze of her eyes they'll see blood
and rubble, the broken children.
On her lips, they'll read...

You supply the name of her city.

The Book Market, Baghdad

We plant trees for those born later
BRECHT

The books are back.
For months, holding their dusty breath
in the dark – under beds,
in cellars – they have waited
for sane enough times.

Now, they have sensed a shift,
an opening for language,
and untidy spillages of books
provisional as healing skin
spread themselves over the ripped paving.

Word flies across the city: books
are reclaiming the streets.
Readers cluster round
the scuffed and lurid colours, hungry
for news that stays news,

for the chance to be transported.
Risk is relative. One bombing daily
means life is almost normal.
In the Souk al-Ghazal caged birds
are changing hands again.

Autumn 2008

II

LOST AND FOUND

Lost is not vanished; nor is it finished

GEOFFREY HILL

Overthrown

Here in the ultimate adventure,
the about-to-happen on the brink of fall,
he'll cheat Death, and its twin tyrant, Time.

He's the grand narrator, master of ceremony,
the thrill of animating this performance
almost climactic. No more diminishment –

no power could be more absolute than his.
He plots his perfect closure, shaping
the final metaphor, from which all follows –

though this poem is literal. It all takes place
in the four stanzas he paces in his head;
its metre is rope, the length of line precise,
its feet those of the chair he'll kick away.

Family Man

He went without saying,
the quiet man in the house opposite,
and with such meticulous forethought
for the sickening surprise
it was a week before she found him,
and then because the grass needed a cut;

and if I hadn't known them,
the family in the house opposite,
it would have been an event on the cusp
between tragedy and the grotesque,
how he'd hidden his briefcase, his good shirt,
tidied the notes for his stand-up routine;

but I saw how she searched
from room to room in the house opposite
as though any minute she might find
an explanation she could live with,
file away, though that's what he'd withheld
like so much else; and I wondered if

in his month-long preparations
the family man in the house opposite,
knowing how one emotion can occlude
another, had devised such cruel arrangements
so she'd pour into the emptiness he'd leave
a bitter sense of grievance, more than grief.

Death Sentences

I hold you on my lap
give you your feed.,
you in your pink jumpsuit
nineteen and shrinking.
I cuddle you, *good girl*.
You take in tiny sucks,
milk with supplements.

Each second you don't throw up
is a tiny chance
for your cells to grasp at,
a tiny puddle of hope
and you know it
and destroy it
triumphant.

I help you into clean pyjamas
you're too weak for.
I'm screaming, silent.
Hatred and love
burst from the same root
tough as knotweed.

I loathe your stranglehold
your yellow eyes
imprisoning me,
knowing exactly how.
Your wrinkled fingers
clutch me by the heart.
Monster. Dear one.

Born too early
you were covered in down;
I laughed at my little swimmer
arrived in a new element.
Now your face
is growing hair again.

Rage, horror interminable.
I can't make you choose life
if even this isn't enough.

Go back to the small
dark death-heaven
you've always wanted.
Let me be free of you.
My love.

Air Baby

In bed, I took care
not to stretch too extravagantly
for fear of smothering him.

I placed him in the supermarket trolley
testing his patience
while I dithered over dips and juices.

He bumped my ribs
as he dangled in a sling in front of me;
our eyes met in adoration –

I could almost see the world
through those blue eyes,
be that vividly astonished.

I loved his tiny strong fists
gripping my forefingers,
his hefted weight

but his head seemed
too heavy on its stalk,
so I made him a few weeks older.

When he began to crawl
I knew the time had come
to take him to the park,

leave him under
a flowering cherry;
walk on.

The Sunday Fathers

You see them in parks,
McDonalds, shopping centres,
neatly pressed children,
well-shaven fathers:
Happy Families with the Mrs missing;
she's a gap in the afternoon.

They watch each other
without seeming to.
Where does the father go
when he's not with them?
They can't imagine him.
They worry without words.

What can the fathers ask?
And how? They don't remember
the names of best friends, teachers.
Did they before? Have they
always got the wrong things right?

They eke the questions out
like spending-money.
They try – how they try!
By evening, all of them are bleak,
exhausted.

It's heartbreak by a thousand monosyllables,
a thinning of the skeleton of love
until it snaps.

Recently

Until recently
her mother died long ago.
Now she hears her in the summer dawn,
a hubbub of triumphant accusations
she can't quite make out.

Until recently
she could have told her friend.
But now she can't find him
in the enfilade of rooms she wanders through
calling and calling.

Soon there will be no recently,
only now;
cheery uniforms
that don't have time,
something peculiar
in her pudding bowl.

Dust

Out of slivers, scraps and flakes from the vast genus of the
        overlooked
the night guard of the McPherson Matthews building is making
        a coat.
He sticks onto a shape of fine black calico the promiscuous bits
        of skin
he tweezes from corners, prises from mirror-frames, mortises
        and cracks,
works them, night after night, into a pearl-grey overcoat, the
        deep cowl
many shades of felted hair. What does he care if this is art, or
        craft, or
spiritual devotion – simply, it is what he does. It has taken
        nineteen years
so far. Curator of the unconsidered, he is intending to be
        cremated in it.

I'd So Much Rather

be eating this *tarte tatin*
than be her
with those naked eyes that might
crinkle into tears or smiles
but don't quite, as she stares
intense, almost wordless

at him
shuffling on his chair, out-gazed,
chain-lighting Gitanes,
forced by embarrassment
into broken sentences
in this encounter on the edge of being
the end or perhaps the start of something –

the station buffet
greasy with hundreds
of past meetings...departures...
which, for this woman, who's been here before,
for this man,
reduce to a worn half dozen possible
highs, troughs, bunglings of love,
inescapable scripts of themselves

which surely, though, could be a rewrite this time
as, now, he rests his hand on the table,
the hand she strokes lightly, slowly,
as his feet, invisible to her,
say it all.

I really would.

On Being Easily Led

It may look as though I'm getting somewhere
but it's self-cancelling.
To.... fro....
she drags and drags me
just so I can stay in the same place
more or less.

She looks down on me.
Sometimes her face seems expressionless;
she's often veiled.
But when she strips naked
I wear a silver ribbon that ripples
all the way to France.

It's a devotion of sorts.
I'll follow her for millennia to come;
she couldn't care less.

The Messenger

They found him by the sea, down Margate way,
wandering about, classy suit soaked through.
Wouldn't speak – not a single syllable to go on
so they brought him in here, obviously.

We're used to strange, but he was –
alien you might say, though he ate OK,
slept, drank, shat like the rest of us. Usually
new ones are jumpy, but he seemed at peace

just watchful. Sometimes you'd see a trace of tears.
How can there be nothing but silence on the tip
of a man's tongue – not even *piss off* or *pass the salt*?
He seemed to manage by not wanting anything.

After a while, we gave him painting things
and he made marks – just shapes and scribbles –
nothing made sense. Every day he'd show us,
as though it was a message, or a question – well

you felt useless – you could see from his eyes
it was important. Star gazer's eyes, flecked
with silver light. *Are you a visitor from outer space?*
I said to him, just to be friendly. Silence, of course.

One day he wasn't there. I still miss him.
I know – you might well ask. But I never saw
anyone so beautiful, so completely harmless.
In my mind, I have a name for him…

The Anthropology of Escalators

Offering a moratorium
between shopping and shopping
the department store escalators,
Up shadowing Down in synchrony
like Escher, slide from floor to floor.

God watches from her table
on the edge of the 7th floor café,
where the view plunges to Ground
and humanity in almost all its variousness
glides silently before her.

She makes a list of things people do
when time's suspended on a moving staircase –
and notices how often couples
hug each other

as if they've woken from a dream of avarice
an enchantment of desire
to find they're not alone,
not anxiously, impossibly glamorous
nor hopelessly perplexed
but ordinary and special and loved.

They touch each other in secret places,
only God seeing them as she looks down
at the never-resting escalators
conveying human cargo up,
or down, to the next circle of heaven.

Clothing Aid

Weeks after, with the last leaves yellow
and coming snow a dryness on the tongue,
the package, shoved from a helicopter,
bursts apart on exit and the sky is dizzy
with angels and the children of angels
puffed out and gaudy, planing down.

The trapped survivors scramble, fight
for scraps of what might be something
nourishing, though they soon see
the harsh joke: flimsy English cast-offs
sundresses, women's shorts, short skirts –
fit only for stuffing cracks.

They wait. They wait by diminishing fires.
The human hand's a puny instrument
with no pick or spade to hearten it,
and this is not the first time the mountains
have breathed the stink of unburied dead,
inclined the sheer indifference of their faces.

Years on, those who are children now
may remember how promising they seemed,
how gorgeous, the outlandish dresses;
and think of this as their first opening
on the vast abundance of a world
they hadn't dreamed could be so godless.

Here and There

On the shady side of Rue Caulaincourt
one of the two local down-and-outs
is taking a leak, shaking a last few drops
off the end of his limp, pink dick,
a small defiant gesture – at us, is it?
before tenderly tucking it away.

This side, I'm eating a *bavette*,
succulent, *à point*.
I eat alone, with perfect manners.
I don't even apply lipstick in public.

From here, his prick looks pale,
sad as a deflated balloon.
All day he drinks, and smiles and talks
to an imaginary friend who understands him.
He needs to piss often.
That is his pitch, and he is king of it.

There's no such thing as a meaningless fact.
He is there.
I am here.
In between, like cool impersonal sleet,
the traffic flows and flows.

Night Train to Bologna

Go because you have the freedom not to.
You've seen so many beautiful cities
they blur like old smoke,
but because those cities are never truly lost,
take the night train to Bologna.

Go for the idea of it – night
a lava-flow through fields, down streets
of silent boxes whose lids protect, conceal.
You've chosen enigma, this transposition
in the no time that is sleep,

chosen to risk the embarrassment of sleep
with strangers, to test what can be trusted,
what can be borne.
Nothing simpler than lying down to sleep,
nothing more at the mercy.

Go for the merciful escape,
to find your different
tongue, more vivacious
and more halting – go
to know the foolishness of being foreign.

Know you must record this, now –
that soon, the *yet to come* that is Bologna
will clutter up with fact and memory.
Travelling on this night train
will never taste the same again

though if you get a taste for it, hooked
on lightness, then you'll take
the night train for Trieste, Kazan,
Novosibirsk... each name more open
than the last; each to be realised, and left.

Lost and Found

1

More than the honeycomb, the marvel
of hexagons; more than the offertory candle
or the inscribed tablet; wax finds its apotheosis
in a Donatello or a Chola masterpiece
and, though provisional, though a mere
understudy for the made-to-last,
it must carry some trace of that glory
after it is fugitive, becoming formless.

2

My lost books are the most beautiful.

1978, imagining the thief's language
as he breaks open my suitcase to find
only books: that shiny red Gorky,

The Old Man and the Sea, stark
illustrations – Sheppard and Tunnicliffe;
the enormous fish,
the old man's immense and simple holding on.

3

Not a leader lost, but naïve hope.

Those exultant pints
when we thought we'd voted in
an honest visionary.

Instead we had Pinocchio man
making himself absolutely clear
through a mouthful of dollars.

Hopeless, we voted him in again.

4

Not always gone for good,
jewels may turn up
after months in the cereal packet
or another
over-prudent hiding-place.

Lost can be all to the good:
favourite earrings hardly missed,
choice simplified.

5

Missing
you're present in the negatives you've left:

silent imprints on the body,
on every cell.

Naming them is risky – can console
or may drag open yearning cavities.

Wait – finally
you'll be discharged from history.

6

Vertigo, seeing a car plated
with my old initials,
a woman driver.

I follow, as if I could overtake
that old life of mine
as it might be now,

park in its driveway,
slip in through the front door.

7

Prisons full of broken thugs, incompetents
who once were new-born, once were boys
hard-wired, like all of us, to hope.

On opening night, 1904,
Wendy agreed to mother Peter Pan,
all the Lost Boys;
and grown men in evening dress
wept and wept.

8

Caricature, the brittle flicker of silent film,
blocks the light.
My lost loves, objects –

what kind of fact have you become?
Dead fact mostly; grey cellophane
scrim over what was green and lovely

though sometimes a dream scorches through
in three dimensions.

9

all very well
for the shepherd
to do his rejoicing number

but what about us
don't we get any credit
for staying where we're put

we're not the ones
who should be sheepish

10

Not on my desk
not in the bathroom cabinet
or on the car roof.

I turn my bed upside down;
not there.

Only because
I was looking through them
could I see so clearly
where they were not.

11

When he was a baby
he was put in the bath tub
with his twin brother
and one of them drowned.

In later life, he'd say
'They thought my brother died,
but I was the one
who drowned that day.'

12

This morning, Vasantha draws
a *kolam* in rice flour
precise, symmetrical,
on the threshold of the house.
    Passing feet scuff it, the wind
    blurs it, crows peck at it,
which is the point.
Tomorrow she will make one again.

13

I took this photograph
to preserve the view of the lake, hills,
the thin man selling coconuts –

but it's not the same.

I can't remember
how it was exactly, but I know
it was different. Perhaps
because he shouted afterwards.

14

Where are our limbs, warts, breasts
and other sliced off parts?

Glass jars, some putrid landfill,

or gone up in smoke
to breeze around the world
as vagrant molecules
randomly re-formed?

We amputees need to ask.

15

Umbrellas, of course,
macs, cigarettes, sandwiches (we bin them)
a Cartier bracelet with an obscene inscription
knickers (quite a few)
wigs, dentures
single shoes
a penis in a bottle (really)
Oh, and a flatpack-coffin catalogue.

16

Three big disappointments:
losing the Junior
Marbles Championship;

finding the Elgin marbles
weren't huge and fabulous
orbs of coloured glass;

and, despite Sudoku,
slowly losing mine.

17

– is that the poem
lost when I sloshed
coffee into my lap
top, then hauled it stuttering
from my living memory

or is it a pale impersonation
of that original, witty, pithy
illuminating thing?

18

Already, certainly,
Death has put the bullet-pointed
items of its agenda
in the post.

But it hasn't yet arrived.
I can still hope to record apologies,
table amendments, any other business.
Press for an adjournment, even.

19

Her last lost lover was un-promising:
now you see him, now
you don't.

Her next to last lost lover was
dysfunctional. She lay entranced
as paint flaked from the ceiling.

Lost lovers were her speciality
until now.

20

But you said...
Oh, 'said'.
Cleopatra probably said the same to Antony
and only when the asp gripped her
in ultimate consummation,
only then, when it was too late,
when it didn't matter anyway
did she know better.

21

There are some mornings
when the instrument
rejects you, strings
refusing to be won
over. Then
nothing but abject patience will do;
no grievance, no despair, simply
attending, letting it have its say.

Life on Mir

They took small fish, to observe
the effects of weightlessness in water.

Goldfish, ordinary on earth, were now
miraculous, their glitter precious currency,
their tiny mouths' O and O a greeting.

So that when they died some men wept,
feeling, as if for the first time,
how grave a life is. Any life at all.

III

SMALL SHIFT

Small Shift

As if a window has unlatched into a crisp morning,
a move, a commitment perhaps, that up to then
has seemed impossible is suddenly straightforward.

It's the kind of shift that stills you when the dishwasher
you hadn't noticed stops its churning, and silence
is a palpable space, not absence only.

Does it seem small because it comes unearned
as grace – as if real change must come from discipline
or violence, so highly do we prize the will?

But a drop of rain can split a boulder; and quanta of news,
infinitely small, can travel across unimaginable
trillions of particles through the web of inter-being.

So some wild creature risks trust, moves, stirring the air
differently; and you, continents away, open your eyes
onto a world where nothing's happened, yet something.

The Day I Knew I Wouldn't Live For Ever

The summer I conquer water, I taste power again
like learning to walk, but this time I'll remember –
being that proud impossible thing, a swimmer;
ecstatic, buoyed up, striking out and out,
swooping with the waves, diving through.

I flip to look back, and the beach is painting-
by-numbers – coloured patches so small I can't tell
which are my family. I was one of those bright dots
and now my space has closed behind me.
I could not exist, and there'd be no difference.

The sea starts to jostle and leer, I've swallowed
knowledge more serious than I knew there was.
This is too vast for me, and I'm swimming hard,
but the dots and patches don't get bigger. No point
shouting, I am invisible – too far out for anything

but keeping on, though without hope, with no
breath, and aching arms. But my life so far
doesn't pass before me like the teacher said, and now
my feet nudge seaweed, and I wade, jelly-legged
and look for our umbrella, and find it.

Nothing has happened. They haven't missed me.
It's cold. My knitted swimsuit is bleeding magenta
into powder blue. My parents set up cricket stumps.
They don't know it's all the same who wins.
The sun makes them cheerful. I am so much older.

That Was Then, This Is Now

Being young was worry about wetness.
Cursed with the wrong flow at the wrong time
we were summer fruits, too juicy for any kind
of comfort, incontinent of sweat, blood, tears.

Red, shaming on the pure white of the sheet
or anxiously missed. Olfactory paranoia,
the embarrassment of armpits slicked
with deodorant, sticky talcumed feet

and always something to cry about –
from a broken nail, or date, to the suffering
of blacks in Alabama; friends scornful
when I sobbed through *Wuthering Heights*.

Now old, dry, neglecting life for art,
what about some compensating flow?
I'd settle for torrents of fertile phrases,
a flood of bloody utterance from the heart.

Mirrored

No time at all
since I watched old women do their faces
with careful moues, with arch half-smiles,
and thought how can they bear it; thought
I'd avoid mirrors, if I were them.

Now I am them,
and know a sort of hardening of the heart
is what it takes,
a swipe of lipstick almost hypothetical
as if this ruin were temporary,
as if to set your face against decay
worked, even a little.

The Seven Stages of Decrepitude

1

You're one of the unthinking fit
sprinting for the bus (though consciously
not tripping). Fine to offer your seat
to the elderly, stand all the way.

2

Men, you notice, have become
slightly more chivalrous than they used to be.

3

You offer your seat to a man on crutches
but he declines.

4

You offer your seat to an ancient Japanese,
she accepts. Three men jump up
to give you theirs.

5

Young women offer you their seats,
you accept.

6

Young and not so young women rise
elbow their way down the crowded bus
calling, pointing to their seats.

7

Arriving at the stop you're seized
and lifted by strong arms on to the bus
installed in a seat despite your protests
(your voice comes out no louder than a shrew's)
and you know it's kind, and will make them
feel good about themselves, only

it's not your bus.

The Comfort in a Rubber Band

How heartening are boundaries,
those consoling categories
beautifully net;

shiny colour-coded files
stacking up in squared off piles,
the completed set;

love letters bundled up, all fires
long dead; each affair requires
time to tell its story;

but when time makes rubber crumble,
letters promiscuously jumble,
it's time to throw them in the humble
bin bag of history.

London Rain

A composition of metallic light,
the sulky greys and beiges of the river
frame the swatch of spectrum colours
the phalanx of overlapping arcs
bobbing over the bridge from Waterloo
where, later, a dazzle of sparklers
dancing in taxi headlights,
the frustrated snarl of engines,
will divide more than ever
homeless from homed and homing.

A frozen film would be a fall-out
of glass, a cruelty of needles.
What next? And then? Romance.
A murder, say. Louche assignations
in the huddle space of bus stops.
A film needn't be a narrative
but on black lacquered roofs
pigeons, hunched Micawbers,
keep an eye on fluent gutters
carrying news to the underworld.

Best is the music of it –
water scales, water harmonies.
In deserted parks, drips fall through
a supplication of leaves, *plip*, *plip*,
like tiny slaps. The drains are singing
in sheer celebration of excess;
the riff of wheels on streaming tarmac –
steel brushes on the taut skin of the city;
and weather's tireless wrists keep it up
day   and night   and day.

The Gaze

is out on the city streets,
patrolling the suburbs, shopping malls.
Inflated and shiny, it's rolling
along station platforms,
alleys, staking out stairwells,
by day, by night,

indifferent to the fear it spreads,
the prickling skin,
thudding heart,
not knowing its own strength
most of the time.
Consciously.

It looks in at a bar or two,
Johnny Dean's, The Bubble Club,
strokes breasts, glosses hair,
lingering on corners
where the light outlines
plump bums in flimsy cotton.

Even where it's not, it knows
it could be, any time –
in control, any place
car in the car park
eyeing the possibles
counting the drinks...

Then it plays the innocent –
watch it saunter off
to the university
clamber up the library shelves,
flatten itself onto the page.
Just an idea.

All Venice Is a Boat

Sway and stagger, high
on intoxicant light
the pitch and swell of water
teaching your muscles
new tricks, blood
finding vertigo.

Even at night, your bed
is finely balanced, tilting
east and back, hair-triggered
between now and then.
In queasy dreams
you tip over the edge.

The *cittadini* stride through
Campo San Barnaba
on their practised sea legs.
That's how you can tell
Venetian from visitor –
that, and the elegance.

Given time, you could
get used to it,
this altered state.
You have to leave, of course,
to settle for the north,
the lowering cloud,

though, back home, it's days
before your inner ear
can believe what it's told,
your body still flexing
with the lurch of the lagoon,
longing for fluidity, that light.

Before

I think of how 'before' can mean earlier
and in the saying of it
have that catch of longing for a time
that never was, except as daydream –
a time tricked out by desire itself.

So a prisoner writes a poem about a Mum
he kids himself he can remember,
and rings it with careful hearts.

Or it can mean later – as the prisoner
remembers a time when the drink,
the rage, the nicking things,
were still before him. Meaning after.

And tells himself his life is still before him,
and plans how he will learn
computers, look for his Mum...

Meanwhile, in the present, he is brought
before the Governor and given solitary
for hitting a screw who wound him up –

so for now he's unhooked from time,
lost in a slippery maze of prepositions,
and will he ever be able to put
one foot,
            one hand,
                        one thought,

before another?

If Time Is This Never

this calm continual spill over
the edge of the steep,
river sliding without tremor
without let, over the lip
and down, and more
coming, and more
time for ever

and if there's no firm having
no preserving
from endless drop away
life's blood
all loves, marvels, falling
no holding them
in the cupped heart
no retrieving

then what sense, what ground
is there? All around
the water moves and moves
land liquefies, all forms
mutate – where are we
whose bones even
are made of time
to stand?

Enough That There Is

the occasional day when there seems no skin around you
and the whole over-weltering world is a come-in come-on
when the sky is a cupola tender as morning glory
and the morning glory's a Schiaparelli dress
and the dress is both work of art and a vanity
and the vanity is a 'yes!' you give yourself
though your self dissolves in a badinage of birdsong
and the songs are spun sugar, confetti and mango flowers
and the scatter of flowers is stirred by the scutter of lizards
and the lizards' twists and rushes are coded words
and the words are planted right at the heart of a poem
and the poem is... the poem is enough.

Appearances

How to describe the shine
and not what's shining?

Not the apple or the copper pan
but the specular shape that floats

on surfaces? Just as much a thing
to the infant, its hand reaching;

and to us, sky-gazing on a clear night
at the moon, thinking we're fascinated

by a solid object, not reflected light.

House of Words

Only by leaning
against each other
weight, counter-weight
do they not fall flat
again and again.

Only like that
can they enclose space
make worlds
and split infinity
again and again.

It needs dexterity
sleight of mind
knowledge of the laws
of construction
to sustain again and again

the illusion of substance;
and it takes focus
to make them stand up,
willingness to begin
again, and again.

Second Chance

When a bloated bluebottle,
the lazy sort that can't be fagged to fly,
crawls on your pillow, you want it gone
naturally, but this one preferred
comfort and company, so I enclosed it
in a tissue and put it in the bin, although
my inner Jain said what makes you think
that's better than squashing it outright
since its chances in the bin are zero?

It niggled me all night, a thought
zizzing in my head, going nowhere,
so when at dawn I fetched the tissue out
took it to the garden, gently unfolded it,
and the bluebottle, heavy and incredulous,
took off like a Lancaster bomber,
I felt blessed with forgiveness. And if
in its short unpopular life it never does
another gladdening thing, it should be proud.

This. And This

Take this wall – practically
solid, and also
a field of whirling energy,
just as this shingled drift of beach
has one flat name
but is also
billions of tiny stones,
each pulsing and unique.

Take this computer,
mirror of mind, that discriminating
architect of difference;
the dance of binaries
reflecting the way we chop the world
lest we be paralysed by wonder.

But take this hand – skin, muscle, bone and
an electrochemical conversation and
what a cello needs to find its voice and
part of me I say goodbye with.

The Indian Ocean knows nothing
of where precisely it becomes the South Atlantic.
Hold my hand long enough
and you won't know where it ends and yours begins.

Nothing this hand does is without consequence.
Take it.

Countdown to Midnight

It's coming in silence, the way an abstraction
takes shape as an image waiting to grow;
it's coming as hope against hope – potential
as infancy, or unmarked snow.

It's a ship of uncertain destination,
a breathing space between promise and dread;
an imperfect cadence, a Chinese whisper,
a codebook no one could hold in their head.

And though the voice of reason grumbles
dates change nothing, and the pledges
the old year offered were paper-thin,
still, to the parliament of wishes –

our blinkered, greedy, quarrelsome
humanity – let New Year come.

NOTES

Memorial: On 10 June 1944, soldiers from the Waffen SS killed almost the entire population of the village of Oradour-sur-Glane, near Limoges, looted, and set fire to the buildings. As a memorial to the dead, and to the way they died, the wrecked village has been left untouched, and a museum built beside it.

Counting: In February 2003, millions of people, all over the world, took to the streets to demonstrate against the US-led invasion of Iraq which they could see coming. The invasion took place on 20 March 2003.

Clothing Aid: This poem was prompted by TV images following the Pakistan earthquake of 2005.

Life on Mir: Mir was the Soviet (and then Russian) space station, which orbited the earth between 1986 and 2001.